Original Title: 101 Strange But True Paddle Tennis Facts.

©101 Strange But True Paddle Tennis Facts, Carlos Martínez Cerdá and Víctor Martínez Cerdá, 2023

Authors: Víctor Martínez Cerdá and Carlos Martínez Cerdá (V&C Brothers)

© Cover and illustrations: V&C Brothers

Layout and design: V&C Brothers

101

STRANGE BUT TRUE

PADDLE TENNIS FACTS

INCREDIBLE AND SURPRISING FACTS

1

Modern paddle tennis was developed in Spain in the 1960s, when a group of friends from the city of Alcoy, in the province of Alicante, adapted a tennis court in a private house to play a variant of tennis that they called "paddle tennis."

It was a racket game similar to tennis, but with a smaller court surrounded by walls and a lower net.

Over time, this sport became popular in other countries, especially in Latin America, where it underwent a series of adaptations and rule changes.

In Argentina, for example, the scoring system of tennis was adopted, while in Mexico, a variant of paddle tennis that included walls became popular.

In the 1980s, paddle tennis began to gain greater popularity in Spain, and specific courts for this sport began to be built.

From there, paddle tennis evolved and specific rules and regulations were established for this sport.

Nowadays, paddle tennis is one of the most popular sports in Spain and in many other countries, especially in Latin America and some European countries.

2

Paddle tennis is always played in pairs, unlike tennis, where there is individual and doubles mode.

In paddle tennis, the pair of players competes against another pair on a rectangular court surrounded by walls.

Playing in pairs is one of the characteristics that make paddle tennis a very social and fun sport.

Communication and coordination between the two players are fundamental to achieve good results on the court.

In addition, the fact that it is always played in pairs makes it possible to establish friendly and companionable relationships with other players, which can be very beneficial for both the practice of the sport and social life.

Although it is true that paddle tennis is not usually played in individual mode, there are some training courts that are smaller and designed for a player to practice on their own or with their coach.

This mode is mainly used to improve technique and game control, and it is not considered an official competition form in the sport of paddle tennis.

3

Paddle tennis has never been an Olympic game.

For a sport to be considered Olympic, it has to meet certain requirements from the International Olympic Committee.

These requirements ask that the sport be practiced in more than 75 countries in 4 continents for the male category, and in 40 countries and 3 continents for the female category.

Paddle surpasses those numbers, as according to the International Paddle Tennis Federation, this sport is already practiced in more than 90 countries worldwide.

However, formalization is needed in all countries, so that consolidation can be found in all Federations.

According to experts, it is possible that paddle tennis may be considered for an Olympic event, but not in the near future.

It is discussed that paddle tennis may have the probability of being chosen for the 2032 Olympic Games.

4

Paddle tennis is a sport that can be practiced by people of all ages and physical characteristics.

Unlike other sports that require great physical fitness, paddle tennis is an activity that can be adapted to different levels of skill and physical condition.

In fact, paddle tennis is an excellent option for those looking for a physical activity that allows them to stay in shape and active without the need for too much intense effort.

Additionally, because it is played in pairs, it is an excellent option for socializing and establishing relationships with other people.

On the paddle tennis courts, people of all ages can be found, from children to older adults.

Children can start practicing paddle tennis from an early age, as long as appropriate rackets and balls are used according to their size and skill level.

Older adults can also enjoy this sport, as the pace of play is less demanding than in other sports and can be adapted to different levels of skill.

Ultimately, paddle tennis is a very accessible and friendly sport for people of all ages and physical characteristics, making it an excellent option for those looking for a fun and social physical activity.

5

It is very similar to tennis, but it is not the same.

The similarity between these sports is very high, both are played with rackets and the objective is to hit the ball so that it reaches the other side of the court.

However, there are very clear differences that make them completely different.

The first of these can be observed in the playing area.

The paddle tennis court is surrounded by four walls, while the tennis court is completely open.

In addition, the sizes of the courts are noticeably different, paddle tennis courts are smaller than tennis courts.

A clear difference can also be seen in the tool used to hit the ball.

There are also differences in rules and playing style.

In paddle tennis, the ball is allowed to bounce once on the court before being hit, and the wall can be used to return the ball, making the game much more tactical and strategic than in tennis.

There is also a volley zone, which is located in the center of the court, which is used to make quick plays and surprise the opponent.

Another important difference is the speed of the ball.

In paddle tennis, the ball is slower than in tennis, which makes the game longer and focuses more on precision than on strength.

In addition, in paddle tennis, the game is mainly played in pairs, which means that communication and coordination with the partner are fundamental to succeed in the game.

6

The first paddle tennis rackets were mainly made of wood, which made them more rigid and heavier.

These rackets were characterized by being much smaller than current ones and having a reduced hitting surface.

Over time, and thanks to the evolution of the sport, paddle tennis rackets began to be made with other more resistant and lightweight materials, such as fiberglass, carbon, graphene, among others.

These materials allow the rackets to be more resistant and durable, while also being lighter and more manageable.

In addition, currently, paddle tennis rackets also include a large number of innovative technologies and designs that improve player comfort, protection, and performance.

For example, some rackets incorporate cushioning systems to reduce vibrations and prevent arm injuries, while others include technology to increase power and precision in hitting.

In short, the evolution of paddle tennis rackets has been constant and has allowed this sport to become one of the most popular today.

The incorporation of more resistant materials and innovative technologies has improved player comfort, protection, and performance, making paddle tennis an increasingly exciting and demanding sport.

7

Enrique Corcuera.

He is considered the father of modern paddle tennis due to his fundamental contribution to the development of this sport.

Corcuera, who was a Mexican businessman and sports enthusiast, built the first paddle tennis courts around a fronton court to prevent ball loss.

Corcuera had a fronton court at his home and was tired of having to go fetch the balls every time they went out of the court.

Therefore, he decided to build walls around the court to prevent the balls from escaping.

When Enrique and his friends realized they could keep playing after the ball bounced off the walls, everything changed.

It was at this moment that paddle tennis emerged as we know it today.

In addition to building the first paddle tennis courts, Enrique Corcuera also designed the first metal racket.

This revolutionized the way paddle tennis was played, as metal paddles were lighter and more durable than wooden ones, allowing players to perform better on the court.

8

The search for lost balls in paddle tennis has generated anecdotes and amusing situations over the years.

–Climbing trees: Occasionally, a ball can get stuck in the branches of a tree near the court. This can lead to comical situations where players attempt to climb the tree to retrieve the ball. Often, there is an atmosphere of laughter and friendly teasing as players strive to reach the ball.

–Searching in thick bushes: If a ball is lost in a dense bush or in a nearby vegetated area, players can find themselves in amusing situations. The search involves rummaging through branches and leaves, and sometimes it's necessary to overcome unexpected obstacles while trying to reach the ball.

–Negotiating with neighbors: On some occasions, lost balls can end up in neighboring properties or adjacent tennis courts. This can result in amusing situations where players have to "negotiate" with the owners of those properties to retrieve their balls. These unexpected interactions can be comical and sometimes include friendly chats between players and neighbors.

–Unusual obstacles: Depending on where padel is played, unusual obstacles can arise during the search for lost balls. From small ponds or water areas to construction sites, players may encounter additional challenges while trying to find their balls. These unforeseen situations can generate laughter and add an element of adventure to the game.

9

Gonzalo Cunqueiro is known as the world's oldest paddle tennis player.

He was born in Spain in 1928 and started playing paddle tennis in 1975, when he was 47 years old.

Since then, he has been passionate about this sport and has played in various competitions over the years.

Cunqueiro still plays to this day, at 92 years old, and has stated in several interviews that paddle tennis has helped him stay in shape and maintain good mental health.

His dedication and love for paddle tennis have made him an inspiration to many players, and they demonstrate that age is not a limit to enjoy this sport.

10

Difference between paddle tennis and tennis balls.

Paddle tennis balls have less pressure, so they bounce less than tennis balls and are slightly smaller.

In addition:

-Tennis ball: must have a uniform surface of white or yellow color. If it has seams, they must be stitchless. Its diameter must be between 6.35 cm and 6.67 cm and its weight between 56.7 and 58.5 grams. The ball's bounce should not exceed 147 cm and should bounce at least 135 cm. The ball's pressure should be 8.165 kg.

-Paddle tennis ball: must be made of rubber in yellow or white color and have a diameter between 6.32 and 6.77 centimeters and a weight between 56 and 59 grams. Its bounce should be between 135 and 145 cm when dropped on a hard surface from about 2.50 meters. The ball should have an internal pressure of between 4.6 kg and 5.2 kg per 2.54 cm².

11

Juan Lebrón is a professional paddle tennis player born in La Línea de la Concepción, Cádiz, in 1995.

He started playing paddle tennis at the age of 8 and began competing in regional and national tournaments at the age of 14.

In 2013, he made his debut on the professional World Padel tennis Tour circuit and has since been one of the most outstanding players of his generation.

In 2019, Juan Lebrón made history by becoming the first Spanish-born player to reach the number 1 spot in the world paddle tennis ranking, a feat he achieved with his partner Paquito Navarro.

Together, they won five tournaments that season and became one of the most successful pairs on the circuit.

In 2020, Juan Lebrón changed partners and started playing with Ale Galán, another of the most outstanding players on the circuit.

Together, they won several tournaments and defended their leadership in the world ranking, becoming the number 1 pair in the world for the second consecutive year in 2021.

Juan Lebrón is known for his aggressive style of play and power in his strokes.

He is considered one of the most promising players in Spanish and world paddle tennis, and is expected to continue being a prominent figure on the professional circuit in the coming years.

12

Hitting with spin is a technique widely used in paddle tennis, which consists of giving the ball a rotation that makes it leave the court in a way that makes it difficult for the opponent to return.

To achieve this effect, the top part of the ball must be "combed" with the racket, in a movement that combines the impact and sliding of the racket on the ball.

There are different types of spins that can be applied in paddle tennis:

- The topspin effect is achieved by hitting the ball with the top part of the racket, following a descending trajectory, which makes the ball spin forward and upward. This effect is widely used in paddle tennis, as it produces a high and fast bounce that makes it difficult for the opponent to return.

- The slice effect is achieved by hitting the ball with the bottom part of the racket, following an upward trajectory, which makes the ball spin backward and downward. This effect is very useful to make it difficult for the opponent to return, as the ball quickly drops when it touches the ground and moves forward.

- The flat effect is used to hit the ball without applying any spin, which allows precise control over the direction and speed of the ball. This effect is very useful to launch the ball towards a specific point on the court without giving the ball an irregular bounce.

It is important to note that to hit with spin, good technique and practice are necessary.

Attention must be paid to the position of the body and racket, as well as the direction and speed of the movement.

Additionally, it is necessary to choose the appropriate moment to apply the effect and not to abuse it, as it can be counterproductive if not applied correctly.

13

When serving, the server can choose the area where they want the ball to bounce on the opposite court.

The objective is to make the bounce as high as possible so that the ball reaches the side wall after bouncing off the back wall.

The ideal place to make the ball bounce is in the so-called "definition area," which is a space located halfway between the service line and the net, and has a length of approximately one and a half meters.

By making the ball bounce in this area, the possibility of the ball reaching the necessary height to pass over the side wall after bouncing off the back wall is maximized.

If the ball bounces too close to the net, it will not have enough space to rise after hitting the back wall, making it difficult to exit through the side wall.

On the other hand, if the ball bounces too far, it will lose momentum and will not have enough speed to pass over the wall.

In summary, the objective is to aim for the definition area so that the ball bounces as high as possible after hitting the back wall, making it easier to exit through the side wall.

14

In paddle tennis, the impact point on the glass can vary depending on the situation in the game and the type of shot being made.

Generally, for a drive shot, it is recommended to hit the ball on the glass closest to the player, known as the "racket glass shot".

This allows the ball to have more speed and angle when passing the net, making it difficult for the opponent to return.

However, in some situations, such as when executing a lob or a drop shot, it may be more convenient to hit the ball against the glass that is farther away from the player, that is, the one that separates the panels.

This allows the ball to have more height and less speed when passing the net, making it difficult for the opponent to respond.

Regarding the lateral position of the shot, it is recommended to hit the ball about two meters from the side wall, as if it is hit too close to the wall, the ball could bounce off it and not rise enough to pass the net.

On the other hand, if it is hit too centered, the ball may not have enough speed and angle to clear the net and be exposed to a counterattack by the opponent.

15

What is a lob?

It is a technical gesture in which, when hitting the ball, it draws a parabola that allows it to rise and surpass the opponent, forcing them to retreat on the court in order to win the net.

Although it is not the only defensive shot, as playing low is also common, paddle tennis is a sport that is tactically focused on winning the net.

And, for that, having good quality in making a good lob is essential.

With a good lob, we aim to make our opponents retreat, regain control of the point, and take offensive positions that will open the door to building the game and a future definition.

It's the "A" in that "A, B, and C" that is paddle tennis for many. Its name is actually a metaphor.

This gesture is based on the aerial projection that the ball makes once it is hit on its lower part, causing it to take an upward and then a downward direction.

16

How to execute a lob?

To perform a quality lob, it is essential to position the body correctly.

We should stand to the side so that we have enough workspace with our dominant arm and coordination with our legs.

The body, not just the hand, will execute this shot correctly.

Once we are positioned to the side, it is crucial to have the paddle already positioned so that we can hit the ball from underneath.

The lob should be executed when the ball is below hip height and up to knee height, always in a forward position relative to the body.

Once we have found the correct position, the impact will be below the ball to make it rise.

The follow-through will come into play, which means projecting the hit until the end with the feeling of pushing the ball upward.

If you think you can execute quality lobs just because you have a good hand, you will make a grave mistake.

To control the height, direction, speed, and depth of the lob, it is essential to use the flexion and extension of the legs.

17

How to position yourself on the paddle tennis court.

If you are playing at the back, both of you need to be at the back, right behind the service line.

If the court you have has five glass panels at the back (common in paddle tennis courts), you need to position yourself at the junction of the last two panels.

Does your court not have as many panels?

Take one step back from the service line and two steps to the side of the side glass wall.

Memorize this position as it will be the standard for most of the shots you make from the back.

If your opponent is serving, this is the position from which you will return, balancing on your feet and returning the serve.

If the opponent moves to the net after the serve, maintain this position to defend yourself.

Your partner will have to be in the same position but on the opposite side.

When to attack?

When you hit a high enough lob that your opponent has to move back to return it.

To position yourself at the net, use the side posts as a reference.

The first post is the one closest to the net, the second is in the middle, and the third is where the side fence meets the glass.

Where to position yourself for a volley?

At the second post, halfway between the service line and the net.

Why?

Because it allows you to cover the back of the court and quickly move up to the net if your opponent hits a drop shot.

If you hit a good shot to the corner, you can move up to the net for a volley, but don't lose your position too much.

18

The rules.

- The objective of paddle tennis is for the ball to pass over the net into the opposing court with a single hit. During the game, the ball can bounce off the walls. The ball can only touch each team's court once.

- The net is 10 meters long and 0.88 meters high in the center, rising to a maximum of 0.92 meters at its ends.

- As for scoring, the game is played in best of three sets. The pair that wins two of the three sets wins the game. The pair that wins the first six games with a difference of two against their opponent is declared the winner of the set. If there is a tie at six games, a tie-break is played, and if there is a tie at one set, the third set can be played until one of the two pairs achieves a two-game advantage over their opponent.

19

The racket for paddle tennis.

It is one of the most important elements for the practice of this sport.

The International Paddle Tennis Federation establishes that the regulation paddle has a maximum length of 45.5 centimeters, a width of 26 centimeters, and a thickness of 38 millimeters.

As for the manufacturing materials, paddle tennis rackets can be made of a wide variety of materials, such as fiberglass, carbon fiber, EVA rubber, foam, Kevlar, graphene, or tungsten.

Each material offers different characteristics in terms of weight, stiffness, power, control, and durability.

One of the most important characteristics of paddle tennis rackets is that they are perforated with holes throughout their central area, with a diameter ranging from 9 to 13 mm.

These holes help reduce air resistance, allowing the paddle to move faster and be more maneuverable.

In addition, the distribution and size of the holes can also influence the characteristics of the paddle, such as power, control, and comfort.

As for the typology of paddle tennis rackets, three main types can be found: diamond, teardrop, and round.

Diamond-shaped paddles have a wider shape at the top, making them ideal for players seeking more power in their strokes.

Teardrop-shaped paddles have a narrower shape at the top and wider at the bottom, making them ideal for players seeking a balance between power and control.

Finally, round-shaped paddles are circular and are ideal for players seeking greater control in their strokes.

20

The paddle tennis court.

It is divided into two halves, separated by a net that is 0.88 meters high in the center and 0.92 meters high at the ends.

The lines that delimit the court include the baseline, sidelines, service line, and the service box line, all with a width of 5 centimeters.

The service line is located 6.95 meters from the net and the parallel service box line is 3 meters away from the net.

The surface of the court can vary, although the most common ones are made of porous concrete, cement, and synthetic grass.

There are also courts made of glass, wood, carpet, and synthetic resins.

The color of the court can be green, blue, or earthy-brown, and there are certain technical specifications for the construction and maintenance of paddle tennis courts to ensure their quality and safety.

21

Since its inception in 2013, the World Paddle Tennis Tour (WPT) is the most important professional paddle tennis championship in the world, with the participation of the best players at the international level.

Between 15 and 20 WPT tournaments are held each year, plus a Master Final in which the best pairs in the ranking compete.

Participating players travel to different cities around the world to earn points and qualify for the Master Final, where only the top 8 pairs in the ranking after completing the season are invited.

Male and female competitions are held.

The first champions of the WPT in history (2013) were the pair formed by Argentineans Fernando Belasteguín and Juan Martín Díaz in the men's category, and the Spanish pair composed of Elisabeth Amatriain and Patricia Llaguno in the women's category.

22

In the beginnings of paddle tennis, there were many pioneering players in Spain who were fundamental to the development of the sport.

-Arturo Jiménez and his brother Carlos, considered the fathers of modern paddle for having designed and built the first paddle tennis court in Mexico in the 1960s.

-José Segimón, one of the best players in the history of paddle tennis and also one of the founders of the Spanish Paddle Federation.

-Javier Arenzana, a very complete player who achieved great success in the 1980s and 1990s.

-Juan Fontán, a very skillful player who dominated the Spanish circuit for many years.

-Alfonso González Allende, another great pioneer of Spanish paddle tennis.

-Luis Nieto, a very talented player who shone in the 1990s.

Currently, paddle tennis has achieved great popularity in Spain and other countries, and has a highly competitive professional circuit.

Some of the most outstanding players on the circuit are:

-Juan Lebrón, a young but very talented player who has achieved great victories in recent years.

-Ale Galán, another young and very complete player who has managed to position himself at the top of the world ranking.

-Fernando Belasteguín, one of the best players in the history of paddle tennis and a reference for many fans.

-Paula Josemaría, a young Spanish player who has been standing out in recent years.

-Mapi Sánchez Alayeto and Majo Sánchez Alayeto, two twin sisters who form one of the most successful pairs in the history of paddle tennis.

23

Paddle tennis is a sport that has experienced great growth worldwide in recent decades.

It is estimated that it is currently played in more than 75 countries on all continents, with millions of players worldwide.

In many of these countries, paddle tennis is considered one of the most popular racket sports after tennis.

Among the countries with the greatest tradition and presence of paddle tennis are especially Argentina and Spain, where the sport is extremely popular and there are thousands of courts and clubs where it is played.

Also in other Latin American countries, such as Mexico, Brazil, Paraguay, Uruguay and Chile, paddle tennis has a great acceptance and more and more people are practicing it.

In Europe, in addition to Spain, countries such as Portugal, Italy, France and the United Kingdom have also experienced great growth in paddle tennis in recent years.

In North America, paddle tennis has gained popularity in countries such as the United States and Canada, while in Asia, the sport is beginning to grow rapidly in countries such as Japan, China, and South Korea.

24

Alejandra Salazar is a professional paddle tennis player born in Madrid, Spain on February 19, 1988.

She is one of the most prominent players on the women's circuit of the World Paddle Tennis Tour and has won numerous titles throughout her career.

Salazar began playing paddle tennis at the age of 13 and quickly stood out for her skills on the court.

In 2007, she made her professional debut on the circuit and has since partnered with several players, including Carolina Navarro and Marta Marrero.

Salazar has won several important titles throughout her career, including the World Paddle Tennis Championship with Spain in 2018 and the World Paddle Tennis Tour title in 2019 with Marrero.

She has also been a runner-up in the circuit on several occasions and has reached number 1 in the world ranking in women's doubles.

Salazar is characterized by her great technique, agility, and speed on the court, which allows her to move with ease and dominate the game in important points.

In addition, she is known for her great competitive spirit and her ability to work as a team with her teammates.

25

Fernando Belasteguín, known as "Bela," is a professional paddle tennis player born in Argentina in 1979.

He is considered by many to be the best paddle tennis player in history due to his extensive record and impact on the sport.

Belasteguín began playing paddle tennis at the age of 12 and was already competing in local tournaments at the age of 14.

In 1995, at the age of 16, he moved to Spain to dedicate himself professionally to paddle tennis.

Throughout his career, he has won more than 180 titles in different tournaments and categories, including 16 World Paddle Tennis Tour titles, 13 World Championship titles, 3 European Championship titles, and 2 Spanish Championship titles.

Belasteguín has been number 1 in the world ranking of the World Paddle Tennis Tour for 15 consecutive years, from 2003 to 2018, making him the player who has held that position the longest in the history of the sport.

He has also been named Best Player of the Year of the World Paddle Tennis Tour on 11 occasions.

In addition to his great skills on the court, Belasteguín is known for his mentality and competitive attitude, which has allowed him to remain in the elite of paddle tennis for so long.

26

Arturo Coello is a Spanish paddle tennis player born in Valladolid on September 22, 2002.

He started playing paddle tennis at the age of 8 and has had a meteoric career since then.

In 2019, at just 16 years old, he won the Absolute Spanish Championship in pairs, becoming the youngest player to achieve it.

In 2020, despite the season being interrupted due to the pandemic, Arturo Coello managed a total of 6 victories in World Paddle Tennis Tour tournaments.

In 2021, Coello formed a pair with veteran Argentine player Fernando Belasteguín, one of the biggest names in the world of paddle tennis.

Together, they have achieved important triumphs such as the Absolute Spanish Championship in pairs and the Estrella Damm Barcelona Master.

But undoubtedly, the most outstanding moment in Arturo Coello's career came in 2022, when at just 19 years old, he became the youngest player in history to win a World Paddle Tennis Tour tournament, by winning the Miami Open alongside Fernando Belasteguín.

This victory earned them both recognition as the revelation pair of the season.

27

Bea González is a Spanish paddle tennis player born in Malaga in 2001.

She started playing paddle tennis at just 7 years old at her local club, Club La Capellanía.

By the age of 12, she was already competing in national and international tournaments.

In 2018, she joined the youth team of the Spanish Paddle Tennis Federation (FEP) and became the Spanish under-23 champion.

In 2019, Bea González made history by becoming the youngest player to win a top-level title in the World Paddle Tennis Tour, the most important professional padel tennis circuit.

She did so at the Madrid Open alongside her partner Martita Ortega.

Since then, she has continued to rise in the world rankings and has established herself as one of the most promising players on the circuit.

Bea González stands out for her fast and aggressive game, with great anticipation skills and a spectacular hit.

She is a very complete player who performs well in all aspects of the game.

In addition to her talent on the court, she is also very popular among fans for her friendliness and approachability.

28

Although paddle tennis is not usually associated with cases of sports fraud, there was a case in 2019 in which two players were sanctioned for attempting to manipulate the outcome of a match in the World Paddle Tennis Tour.

The players, Federico Chingotto and Juan Tello, were accused of not playing at their maximum effort in a match against Pablo Lima and Fernando Belasteguín at the 2019 Master Final.

The suspicion of fraud arose when it was observed that Chingotto and Tello played several points without moving much, and lost the match in straight sets.

The Competition Committee of the World Paddle Tennis Tour determined that Chingotto and Tello had violated the tour's code of conduct and imposed a financial penalty and a suspension from two tournaments.

The sanction was very controversial at the time, but the World Paddle Tennis Tour defended its decision to sanction the players for not complying with the sportsmanship and ethics of the sport.

29

Marta Ortega is a Spanish paddle tennis player born on October 16, 1996, in Madrid.

She began playing paddle tennis at the age of 6 and at the age of 14, she moved to Barcelona to train at the CAR (High Performance Center).

Since then, she has been one of the most outstanding players on the professional paddle tennis circuit.

Martita Ortega, as she is known in the world of paddle tennis, has won several important titles in her career, including the Absolute Spanish Championship in 2014 and 2017, the Paddle Tennis World Team Championship in 2014 and 2016, and several World Paddle Tennis Tour (WPT) titles, including the Spanish Championship in 2016 and the World Championship in 2018.

In addition to her success in paddle tennis, Martita Ortega is also known for her beauty and style, which has made her a popular figure on social media.

She has also been the face of several fashion and sports brands.

Currently, Martita Ortega plays in the women's professional paddle tennis circuit of the World Paddle Tennis Tour, forming a pair with the Spanish player Ariana Sánchez.

Together, they have achieved important victories in tournaments and are among the most outstanding pairs in the circuit.

30

What racket to buy to start playing padel tennis?

If you buy a cheap racket, it will probably only have some fiberglass and foam inside.

Normally, you will need a slightly better tool.

You don't have to spend more than 300 euros on a paddle, but you should invest in the mid-range, as paddles over 300 euros are designed for professional players and are so hard that you will probably injure yourself playing with them.

The ideal price for a beginner's paddle is between 100 and 200 euros.

Soft and not too heavy: there are plenty of paddles in that mid-soft range.

31

How to choose paddle tennis shoes?

First, don't play paddle tennis with your running shoes: they don't have lateral reinforcement and slip on the court, which can cause you injury.

If possible, look for shoes with a herringbone sole.

If you can't find them, tennis shoes for all types of terrain will work, especially if there isn't much sand on your paddle tennis court.

What about sand?

The first paddle tennis courts used to have a lot of sand on the surface, and that's where the herringbone sole is most noticeable, as it has more grip, but modern courts don't have as much sand and a tennis shoe for all types of terrain should work well.

32

What grip tape to use for paddle tennis?

When you buy a racket, it comes with a standard grip tape, usually quite small.

If you are a man or have large hands, it is better to put a couple of more grip tapes on top.

Keep in mind that, although in tennis there are different grip sizes, in paddle tennis the size is unique, so you have to play with different amounts stacked on top to find your ideal size.

There are many different textures: more sticky, drier, normal, professional... each brand has its own models.

Choose one, try it on, see if it's comfortable for you, put another one on top if you want to feel the grip a bit thicker, take it off if you prefer it thinner...

And something that is sometimes overlooked is the usefulness of having a protection that comes on the outer top of the racket.

Many beginners don't realize that paddles wear out sometimes on the edge and with a protector, it is less likely to happen, especially if you have spent a lot of money on the racket.

However, a protector adds weight to the top of the paddle, so you will have to get used to it, but putting grip tapes on the handle can be the ideal counterweight when balancing your paddle.

33

The number 1 mistake that paddle tennis players should not make.

From the back of the court, do not go directly to the net to attack.

It is something that many players do even after returning the serve: they return the serve and go to the net.

It's true that one of the objectives of paddle tennis is to occupy the net position because it's easier to finish with a winning point from there, but that doesn't mean you have to go up immediately: you have to know how to choose the ideal moment to go up.

A good moment: you receive an easy ball, you hit a lob to the back of the court, above your opponents, and take the opportunity to move up while they go back to return it.

This way, you take fewer risks and it's less likely that you'll make a mistake.

It's better to do this than to do it after a volley in no man's land.

34

Reading your opponent's game is a very important skill in paddle tennis because it allows you to anticipate their movements and have a tactical advantage.

To read your opponent's game, it's important to pay attention to their playing style, the type of shots they use, and their position on the court.

At the beginning of the game, it's important to observe your opponent's movements to understand their playing style.

Additionally, pay attention to the errors they make and the areas of the court where they struggle the most.

As the game progresses, it's important to adjust your strategy to take advantage of these weaknesses.

It's also important to read your opponent's intention before they hit the ball.

Observe their position on the court, the direction of their gaze, how they hold their paddle, etc.

These clues can help you anticipate their movements and position yourself correctly on the court.

35

When you move up to the net in paddle tennis, it's important to consider some tactics to maximize your chances of winning the point.

An effective tactic is to try to hit the ball towards the corners, making it harder for your opponent to respond with an effective return.

Additionally, it's important to position yourself near the net and in a central position, which will allow you to cover more space and have more options to intercept the ball.

When you're at the net, you should also be attentive to your opponents' movements and possible returns.

Try to anticipate their shots and move quickly to intercept the ball.

Another effective tactic is to try to keep the ball low, making it harder for your opponents to respond with an effective return and giving them less time to prepare their shot.

36

How to subtract when they serve to the middle?

When subtracting, there are a couple of things you should consider, and you should also take into account how your opponents are positioned on the court, whether they are in Australian formation (both on the same side of the court) or in normal formation (one on each half of the court).

If they are in normal formation, it's logical to try to return the serve to the player who hit it, but if they are in Australian formation, you have to avoid the temptation to return to the empty half of the court, as that is exactly what your opponent expects: the player who served quickly moves to the free side to occupy it and move up to the net.

What to do?

Hit a lob directed to the side of the court from which you are receiving.

37

How to return a serve that goes to the T?

If they serve right to the T (the back line, middle area), and you move to the middle to hit hard, you will leave your zone unoccupied and be out of position, so they can easily send the ball to the corner to leave you out of action.

That's why the best decision if they serve towards the T is to hit a lob, which will allow you to gain a little more time to get into the right position.

That lob will also allow your partner to move up to the net and become more aggressive.

If, on the other hand, the ball is easy and you have sufficient skill level, you can try to hit a lob or return it to the feet of the player who made the serve, which will put you in an attacking position and put them under pressure.

38

How to subtract if the serve goes towards the glass?

If the serve comes lifted against the glass and you don't think you can hit a good lob, it's best to return it low, hitting it, if possible, below your shoulder so that it's difficult for them to attack, which will put you in a neutral position at that point and start gaining ground.

In short, it's interesting to maintain a conservative position with difficult serves, since a returned ball can help you stay in the game and have the possibility of winning the point.

Depending on the serve, choose one option or another to subtract to win more points.

39

Extra tips for returning your opponent's serve.

- Try to find a pattern in your opponents' serves: a player will feel more comfortable if a serve works for them and unconsciously they will tend to look for that serve, especially if things are going badly.

- Analyze the risk and reward: although everyone loves to hit a winning return, think if it's worth complicating things when sometimes it's enough to just pass the ball.

- If you feel confident, look for your opponent's backhand volley: it's a difficult shot to make, especially right after a serve.

- If your return is powerful, your opponent will probably only be able to get the ball off their racquet and return it softly, which puts you in a clear advantage to dominate the point.

40

Properly warming up before a paddle tennis match is essential to prevent injuries and perform at your best.

The duration of the warm-up may vary depending on the player and weather conditions, but it's generally recommended to dedicate between 10 and 15 minutes to warm up properly.

The warm-up should include joint mobility exercises, dynamic stretches, cardio exercises, and some typical paddle tennis shots, such as the serve, volley, and smash.

It's important to emphasize the muscles and joints that are most used in paddle tennis, such as the shoulders, elbows, wrists, legs, and ankles.

During the warm-up, it's important to pay attention to bodily sensations and not to force movements excessively.

It's also recommended to hydrate properly before, during, and after the match, as well as to wear comfortable and appropriate clothing and footwear for playing paddle tennis.

41

Some tricks for serving like a professional in paddle tennis:

- **Ball bounce**: Professional players bounce the ball in front of them and to the side of the stroke to be able to balance themselves and have a better position for the serve.

- **Racquet position**: Although the stroke will be made from the front, professionals take the racquet all the way back to get a greater swing and more power in the serve.

- **Impact height**: Professional players hit the ball around waist height and never near the ankles, as this allows them to have better control over the serve.

- **Spin**: When serving, professional players try to cut the ball a little to give it a slice, which makes it more difficult for their opponent to return.

- **Follow through**: A professional player always follows through and moves towards the net to be in a better position to perform the volley that will come after.

42

Using the walls in paddle tennis is one of the fundamental skills that every player must acquire.

When the ball hits the wall, its trajectory can change, and this can be used to our advantage to surprise the opponent.

There are different ways to use the walls in paddle tennis.

One of the most common is to hit the ball on the side or back wall so that it acquires a different trajectory and deceives the opponent.

The wall can also be used to recover difficult balls that are very close to it by hitting them with a soft and precise touch.

Another technique is called the "three-wall shot".

It consists of making a powerful shot of the ball towards one of the side walls, so that it bounces and returns to the court, which makes the opponent have to make a greater effort to reach the ball and make their return.

43

More skill than strength.

Hitting the ball across the court as many times as possible can be very satisfying.

The sound of the racket, the quick bounces, the opponents (who are also new to the court) giving it their all...

But paddle tennis is not a game of strength, in fact, excessive strength can cause problems and be counterproductive.

Timing a smash is crucial to score more points.

There are plays that require maximum strength, but only a few.

Start by learning to control the ball before focusing on developing your paddle tennis strokes!

44

Playing as a team is essential in paddle tennis, as it is a doubles sport.

In addition to finding a partner who has a similar level to yours, it is also important to have good communication and synergy with him or her.

In team play, it is important to cover the spaces on the court well and know when to advance to intercept the ball and when to stay at the back to defend.

It is also important to have a good game strategy and work as a team to execute it correctly.

It is essential to avoid clashes between teammates, as this can negatively affect performance and the atmosphere on the court.

Fun and enjoyment of the game should always be a priority.

It is also important to respect each player's turn to serve and have good communication to avoid confusion on the court.

Playing as a team not only improves sports performance but also fosters companionship and friendship.

45

The "More than one ball" tactic in paddle tennis refers to the strategy of playing several balls in the same point instead of waiting for the opponent to return a single ball.

This tactic can be very effective in certain situations of the game, but it also has its risks.

As mentioned, one of the main advantages of playing more than one ball is that it can increase pressure on the opponent and give them more opportunities to make mistakes.

Additionally, playing several balls can also be beneficial for player practice and improving their coordination on the court.

However, playing more than one ball can also be risky, as it can give the opponent more opportunities to take control of the point.

For example, if you play a short ball and the opponent returns it, you may not be well-positioned to respond to the next ball.

Therefore, playing more than one ball requires good communication and coordination between players, to ensure that both are in the right position to respond to each ball.

46

"Playing on both sides" is a commonly given advice in paddle tennis, and it refers to the importance of being able to play in both positions on the court, that is, both on the right side and on the left side.

This is especially important for players competing at the intermediate and advanced level, as it allows them to adapt to different situations and playing pairs.

When a player is able to play on both the right and left sides, they can have a better understanding of what it takes to succeed in each position, making them a more versatile player capable of adapting to different playing pairs.

Additionally, this can also help improve communication between players and their ability to make decisions as a team.

It is important to note that while it is recommended to be able to play on both sides, each player generally has a preferred position that better suits their skills and playing style.

Therefore, it is important to practice in both positions and work on developing skills to improve as an overall player.

Materials.

Paddle rackets can be constructed from different materials, which greatly influence their weight, behavior, and performance.

Here are the main compositions:

-Carbon. Offers greater lightness, strength, and stiffness.

-Fiberglass. More flexible, but less light. Improves impact resistance when mixed with graphite or carbon. Due to its flexibility, it is ideal for placing on the impact surface of the racket. Allows for total ball output at all times, which is useful for beginner or mid-range rackets.

-Graphite. Very light and resistant, used as reinforcement in areas of the racket such as the frame, torsion zones, and heart.

-Titanium. It is usually applied in powder form mixed with paint. Provides firmness and resistance without excessively increasing the weight of the racket. Provides greater durability.

-Kevlar. Resistant fabric that is added as additional reinforcement in areas of the frame or in the racket face. Considerably increases the durability of the racket.

-Composite. Resin material composition used to strengthen the structure of the racket.

-Epoxy. Liquid and dense resin that is applied to all the fibers that make up the racket. Makes the racket a homogeneous block. It is also applied to varnish and paint additives to make them more resistant and waterproof.

-Foam Rubber. It is the most recommended rubber for players looking for a softer touch. Prevents the player from experiencing wrist, elbow, or shoulder pain.

-Eva Rubber. It is a more powerful, denser rubber.
It comes in various densities, from softer to harder.

48

Questions for Ale Galán.

-What do you like most about being a professional player? And the least?

That my passion is my job, in both cases. I feel very fortunate that it is so, but on the other hand, I think that at times I don't enjoy it as much as I should. In the end, it stops being your hobby.

-Do you have any quirks or rituals on the court before or during a game?

I always let the opponent choose heads or tails before starting the games (laughs). Then, sometimes, I am repetitive during some tournaments. If I start the first day doing something, then I repeat it every day, like going in the same position in the car and things like that (laughs).

-What do you think are the keys to success?

Daily work, perseverance, and determination. Determination is very important to me. It was instilled in me when I was 16 years old and started focusing 100% on paddle tennis, and I have had it since then.

49

In paddle tennis, balls are a fundamental element of the game and it is important to ensure that they are in the best condition to guarantee a fair and high-quality competition.

In official matches, a rule is established in which the balls must be changed every 9 games, which means that after 9 full games have been played (i.e. 18 games in total), new balls must be used.

The reason behind this ball change is that, with use and wear, the balls lose pressure and their bouncing ability decreases.

This can affect the outcome of the game, as players may find it more difficult to control the ball's bounce and perform certain strokes.

Additionally, by regularly changing the balls, it ensures that both teams have the same playing conditions and eliminates the possibility of one team having an advantage by playing with newer and better-conditioned balls.

It is important to note that this rule only applies to official matches, such as those in the World Paddle Tennis Tour, and not necessarily in informal or training matches.

In these cases, players may decide when to change the balls based on the conditions and their own judgment.

50

According to the regulations of the World Paddle Tennis Tour, the maximum thickness allowed for a paddle tennis racket is 38 mm, measured at the widest part of the racket.

If a referee suspects that a racket may be outside the established limits, they may conduct a control of it.

In the event of a control being carried out on the racket, a tolerance of 2.5% in its thickness with respect to the regulations is allowed, which means that the racket cannot exceed 38.95 mm in thickness.

Additionally, other technical aspects of the racket are checked, such as its weight, shape, roughness, and flexibility.

It is important to remember that any modification or manipulation of the racket to alter its characteristics is prohibited and may be considered a serious offense.

Therefore, players must ensure that they use approved rackets that comply with the regulations' specifications to avoid being penalized.

51

The regulations of the World Paddle Tennis Tour state that balls used in official matches must be yellow or white in color, so balls of other colors are not allowed.

This is because these two shades provide the best visibility for players and spectators in different lighting conditions.

Additionally, balls used in matches must comply with certain technical specifications regarding their size, weight, and bounce.

For example, the ball's diameter must be between 6.35 and 6.77 centimeters, its weight must be between 56 and 59.4 grams, and its bounce must be between 135 and 145 centimeters when dropped from a height of 2.54 meters.

The use of balls that do not meet these technical specifications can be penalized if detected, and could affect the development of the match and the performance of the players.

52

In paddle tennis, a player can hit the ball into the opponent's court if certain conditions are met.

Firstly, the ball must have bounced in their own court and hit the walls before returning to the court they launched it from.

If this is fulfilled, the player can hit the ball as long as they or their paddle haven't touched the net, its posts, or the opponent's court before hitting it.

This type of shot is known as an "attack volley" or "smash volley" and is generally used as a strategy to surprise the opposing team and win points quickly.

However, it is a risky play and should only be used in appropriate situations, as an error can result in a loss of point.

53

The schedules of paddle tennis matches must be respected, and it is the player's obligation to inform themselves of them.

Additionally, it is important to arrive at the court with enough time to prepare adequately before the match and avoid unnecessary delays.

In some tournaments, if a player arrives late to their match, they may lose the right to play and be disqualified.

It may also happen that if a match is delayed for too long, the tournament organizer decides to shorten the playing time to be able to continue with the scheduling of the following matches.

Therefore, it is important to respect the schedules to avoid inconvenience and ensure that all matches can be played without problems.

54

In paddle tennis, the order of play refers to who begins serving and on which side of the court the players start.

According to the World Paddle Tennis Tour regulations, the order of play is decided by drawing lots, and in the case of a tie, it is determined by drawing lots again.

However, in some cases, it may be necessary to change the order of play, such as when one of the players arrives late or there is some other circumstance that justifies it.

In these cases, the express authorization of the tournament's referee is required.

It is important to note that the change of order of play can only be made before the match starts, and once started, it cannot be modified without the authorization of the referee.

Additionally, any change must be notified to the players and the audience present.

55

The equipment of a paddle tennis team is important, as it can help create a sense of unity and belonging to a group.

In team tournaments, each player usually wears their own clothing, but it is recommended that team members wear similar gear to be easily identifiable as part of the same team.

However, it is not mandatory for players to wear the same gear, as each player has the right to choose their own clothing.

Some teams choose to wear shirts or polos of the same color or with the same designs to differentiate themselves from other teams, while others prefer each player to choose their own clothing.

In any case, it is important that players feel comfortable and confident in their clothing to perform at their best in the competition.

56

Paddle tennis is a sport that offers numerous physiological and psychological benefits.

Some of the most prominent physiological benefits include:

- **Increased muscular strength:** As a sport that involves quick and explosive movements, paddle tennis is an excellent training to improve muscular strength and endurance.

- **Improved general and specific coordination (hand-eye):** Padel requires great coordination between upper and lower extremities movements, which helps improve both general and specific coordination.

- **Active habit in physical activity practice:** Paddle tennis is a fun and challenging physical activity that can help people stay active and committed to a healthy lifestyle.

- **Fighting obesity and sedentary lifestyle in the child population:** In recent years, obesity and sedentary lifestyle in the child population have become increasingly common problems. Paddle tennis can be an excellent option to fight against these issues, as it is a fun physical activity that can be practiced in a team.

- **Caloric expenditure and appropriate mood states:** As a physical activity that combines intense movements with rest periods, paddle tennis is an excellent way to burn calories and improve mood. Playing paddle tennis releases endorphins, which helps reduce stress and anxiety.

57

Paddle tennis also has multiple psychosocial benefits.

Some of them are:

-Reduces stress and anxiety: Paddle tennis can help reduce stress and anxiety by releasing endorphins, hormones that reduce pain and improve mood.

-Improves self-esteem and confidence: Paddle tennis can improve self-esteem and confidence by providing a sense of achievement and success when goals are achieved and skills are improved.

-Encourages sociability and teamwork: Paddle tennis is a sport played in pairs, which encourages sociability and teamwork. Players must communicate and coordinate to win the game.

-Stimulates concentration and mental agility: Paddle tennis requires a lot of concentration and mental agility to be able to follow the trajectory of the ball and make quick decisions.

-Improves discipline and perseverance: Paddle tennis requires discipline and perseverance to improve skills and techniques in the sport. Constant practice and dedication are key to achieving a good level in this sport.

-Develops empathy and conflict resolution skills: As a team sport, paddle tennis can help develop empathy and effective conflict resolution skills, as players must learn to communicate and collaborate to achieve success.

58

Playing paddle tennis can involve some risk of injury, especially if warm-up and stretching exercises are not performed properly before and after the game.

Some common injuries associated with paddle tennis include:

-Shoulder injuries: Due to the repetitive movement of hitting the ball and the high speed of the game, shoulder injuries such as tendinitis or bursitis are quite common in paddle tennis players.

-Back injuries: Intense physical activity and repetitive movements can cause back problems, such as muscle contractures, herniated discs, or lower back pain.

-Knee injuries: Knees are also an area that is frequently affected in paddle tennis, especially in players who have incorrect technique or make sudden and abrupt movements. The most common knee injuries are patellar tendinitis or inflammation of the goosefoot tendon.

-Foot injuries: Paddle tennis is a sport that requires a lot of lateral movement and jumping, so it is common for players to suffer foot injuries, such as ankle sprains, plantar fasciitis, or blisters.

-Wrist injuries: Wrists can also be affected in paddle tennis, especially in players who have incorrect technique or use an inadequate paddle tennis. The most common wrist injuries are tendinitis and epicondylitis.

It is important to take preventive measures to avoid these injuries, such as using appropriate equipment, warming up before the game and stretching after it, and having a good game technique. In case of pain or injury, it is recommended to consult a doctor or physiotherapist.

59

Regarding the age to start practicing paddle tennis,it is recommended to start from 4 years old, but ideally it should be adapted to each child according to their individual abilities and characteristics.

It is important to consider that, at early ages, the goal is not so much to teach the game technique, but to develop psychomotor skills and eye-hand coordination.

Therefore, in classes for children of these ages, games and exercises that encourage these skills can be used, and gradually introduce the technique of paddle tennis.

It is recommended that classes for children be fun and dynamic, so that they do not lose interest and motivation for the sport.

Additionally, it is important to respect the times and rhythms of each child, and allow them to enjoy the game without excessive pressure or demands.

60

Everything to the weaker opponent.

The opposing team consists of a skilled player who never misses and another who is having a bad day or is not up to the task.

Therefore, we focus on sending all shots to the same player, achieving a double objective:

- The "bad" player misses and we earn points.

- The "good" player is left cold and does not get into the game.

This often comes with a kamikaze ball-stealing effect from the "good" player who realizes the situation (probably because they do the same) and tries to hit one, failing by coming in late and poorly, aggravating the problem.

61

I did not come to fight against the elements.

Paddle tennis is not played in a bubble and often not even indoors.

Sometimes the sun or strong gusts of wind are annoying, which are taken advantage of by sneaky players.

Does the sun shine directly in one side of the court?

Then, hit all lobs.

The opponent looks up and finds a bright yellow ball that, unlike the bright yellow paddle tennis ball, can cause blindness if looked at directly.

This is a very effective tactic that has cemented great victories.

From here, we recommend not abusing it, mainly because the opponent will ask to change sides in odd games, and we will be the ones receiving spoonfuls of our own medicine.

62

Playing with armor.

There are a series of players with reflexes who always know how to place the racket at the precise moment no matter how fast and strong the ball goes.

It is precisely these kinds of players who drive paddle tennis players crazy who finish off a good ball thinking they will not return it.

The solution against human frontons is very simple: target shooting.

When shooting, one does not place the racket to return the ball, but to safeguard their vital organs in this order: genitals, genitals, and face.

The experienced sneaky player already knows where to aim to ensure victory.

This is one of the most shameless dirty tactics, no matter how many times one apologizes, one, two, or three hundred and fourteen times, the opponent will not hesitate to put it into practice once again.

When it gets to this point, we recommend wearing dark clothes where bloodstains are not noticeable: we cannot give clues of our weakness to the opponent.

63

Psychological abuse.

Paddle tennis is not only a confrontation of technique
and physicality, but also a mental duel.

Here, especially manipulative players have an advantage
to undermine the morale of a weak opponent.

The psychological menu can start with indirect
hints and veiled threats during warm-up.

If there is confidence, one can insult directly.

The techniques of this type are varied and very creative:

- Tasteless point celebrations.

- Singing balls out with sarcasm.

- Nicknaming players, their shots or playing style.

- Pure and hard cynicism when apologizing for
a lucky shot.

- Regretting that one is shooting at the opponent.

We remind you that the tone and intensity of these
methods depend on the confidence one
has with the opponent.

64

I am my own referee.

Unless we operate in professional environments, referees in paddle tennis are absent.

Therefore, someone has to keep track of points and call out balls that go out.

In civilized sports, there would be no problem, but in the sneaky paddle tennis, it is an inexhaustible source of conflicts.

There are 2 conventions:

- Both pairs keep score and each pair is responsible for calling balls on their side. Unfortunately, illiteracy is a serious scourge of paddle tennis, and only one player of the four on the court usually keeps score, who, if sneaky, will not hesitate to "take" a point while counting. This would not be a problem if opponents realized that each score is taken at the same location on the court, making cheating more difficult.

- Then there is the blatantly calling bad balls good and saying cynically: "I saw it bad, but if you want we can repeat it." The most shameless have even made up rules to deceive their illiterate and unsuspecting opponents. The solution is clear: keep score and know the rules.

65

Paddle tennis Noise.

Playing paddle tennis at any level, whether it's casual or professional, requires a minimum level of concentration to win a match.

A sneaky paddle tennis player will try to disrupt their opponent's concentration with various techniques, the most common falling into the category of "noise and variations."

They can scream after each shot, their own or, if they're a real jerk, after their opponent's shots.

The screams can be of any type: grunts, roars, or Sharapova-style orgasmic moans (generally it's better to abstain from making them in non-mixed matches, because of what people might say).

They can also call the balls out before they reach their target, showing off and bragging about having their own "hawk eye," whether it's with the balls they are supposed to receive or, being a pro jerk, with their own balls that land on the opponent's court, calling them out, even if they are not out, to make their opponent overconfident.

66

The Dark Side of paddle tennis Shot.

Here, in an exercise of masochism and malice in equal parts, the player offers themselves to be the victim of their opponent's paddle tennis anger.

They combine sneaky tactics such as psychological abuse or ostensible gestures like a handball goalkeeper, so that when the opponent has to hit the ball, they only see the face of their annoying opponent mocking them, and they hit the ball to the moon or someplace farther away.

The player who intends to engage in such provocations must be agile and have good reflexes, or else their physical integrity will be in serious danger.

67

What were the paddle tennis courts like?

Paddle tennis courts, at their beginnings, were wall courts.

There were no glass courts.

Glass was introduced when the Professional Circuit began to gain followers in Argentina, and it was used to build stands in the backgrounds and sides so that spectators could watch the matches.

In Spain, until the year 2000, the vast majority of the courts were wall courts, and matches were played on these courts in the professional circuit until recently.

In fact, Juan Martín Díaz and Fernando Belasteguín lost their unbeaten streak of 1 year and 9 months in a Paddle Tennis Pro Tour tournament in 2007, on a wall court against Cristian Gutiérrez and Seba Nerone.

Also, during this time, it was common to find paddle tennis courts made of cement or tennis-quick.

The truth is that the risk of injury on this surface was very high, and soon artificial grass began to be used as the playing surface.

68

Differences between glass and wall.

Wall tracks are usually slower, while glass offers a faster bounce.

In these tracks, where the fence ended and the wall began, there was a protrusion or "peak" that players tried to hit to win the point.

At that time, the rackets were made of wood, the game was slower, and finishing a point was difficult.

Aiming for the "peak" was a widely used option back then.

Antonio Ochoa was a great paddle tennis player who had a special ability to hit the "peak".

Playing against him on those tracks was a nightmare, as he was able to hit the "peak" more than 10 times in a row.

69

"Serve and Stay Back" is an old rule in paddle tennis in Argentina in which the serving team could not move forward to the net, while the receiving team could do it.

This rule led to a very different game than the current one, as the serving team had to remain at the back of the court and defend until the opposing team made a mistake.

In Spain, this rule was never implemented, but in Argentina, it remained until the 90s.

This rule radically changed the game of paddle tennis, as the serving team did not have the possibility of taking the net, giving the advantage to the receiving team to attack and win points.

However, this rule also had the advantage that the serving team could work on their defense and play from the back of the court, and the receiving team had to be more precise with their shots to win points.

Paddle tennis player Juan Martín Díaz, one of the most successful in the history of the sport, began his career in Argentina and played under this rule in some tournaments.

Currently, "Serve and Stay Back" is no longer practiced in Argentina or any other country where paddle tennis is played.

70

"Going out of the court".

Going out of the court to return the ball to play
when the opponent hits it out of bounds by
3 meters is something relatively recent.

The initial rules of paddle tennis were ordered
with two variations, the fence up to 3 meters and
the fence up to 4 meters high.

In Spain, at the beginning, there were few courts
with a fence only up to 3 meters, and hitting
it out by 4 meters is much more difficult.

In any case, going out through the gate and
returning the ball was more difficult before.

The clubs had less space between courts to be
able to go out, and the court doors were much
narrower and did not have protections like
those of now, which are designed to favor
play outside the court and the spectacle.

According to Mago Sanz: "Back then, going out to
return a ball outside the court was almost a feat."

He was the first player who did it.

71

Carolina Navarro.

The woman from Malaga is considered the
best paddle tennis player in history.

She was possibly the first "modern" paddle tennis player and
one who set the standard for an entire generation.

In a time when materials were different and women's paddle tennis
was slower and more defensive, Carolina started "hitting hard".

She was the first to start hitting strong smashes,
her favorite shot, revolutionizing women's paddle tennis.

Her sports record is impressive:

- 9 years as Number 1 in the World.

- 12 years as Champion of Spain.

- 3 times World Champion in pairs (2000, 2006 and 2012).

- 4 times World Champion in Teams (1998, 2000, 2010, 2014).

- European Champion in pairs and in Teams (2019).

- More than 100 professional tournaments won.

- Bronze Medal for Sports Merit awarded by His Majesty King
  Juan Carlos I.

- Sports Merit Medal awarded by the F.E.P.

- Otiñano Trophy for Values 2013.

- Gold Medal of the Province of Malaga 2015.

72

How did Navarro start playing paddle tennis?

When she decided to quit tennis in order to study, Carolina Navarro still had the competitive itch.

At that time, she was giving tennis lessons to some students and a friend of her brother told her about a new sport with similar characteristics to tennis.

She decided to try it and soon fell in love with paddle tennis, which had the great advantage that she could combine it with her studies.

This is how she started, competing locally in Malaga with her sisters Elsa and Belén and, shortly after, at the national level.

The first call she received to compete at the national level was from Ester Muñoz, a player from Madrid.

With very few tournaments, she began to demonstrate her enormous talent and potential and received a call that marked her history a bit and made her very excited: María Silvela, who was then the number 1 player in the ranking.

From that moment on, her progression became unstoppable.

73

According to the official regulations, a paddle tennis court has a length of 10 meters and a width of 20 meters.

However, the outdoor play area, that is, the space surrounding the court, is limited to a zone 2 meters wide, 4 meters long, and 3 meters high.

This means that if a ball goes out of bounds and there are no obstacles outside, players can try to return it as long as they do so within the 10-meter length of the court and without going out of the allowed outdoor zone.

In the World Paddle Tennis Tour, which is the professional paddle tennis circuit, it is common to see players leaving the court to try to retrieve balls and keep them in play.

Some players have exceptional skills in this aspect and are able to reach balls far away from the court.

74

Outdoor play behind the back of the court is a rare situation in paddle tennis, especially in amateur play, but it can occur in the professional arena.

Regarding the regulations, article 13.c)1 of the International Paddle Tennis Federation Regulations states that "a shot is valid if the ball is played within the boundaries of the playing court, without touching any structure or accessory outside the court."

Therefore, if a ball is hit behind the back of the court, players cannot rescue it since they would be out of bounds, which would be considered a fault.

It is important to note that this rule only applies in the case of outdoor play behind the back of the court, as in other cases, playing the ball is allowed as long as it does not touch any structure or accessory outside the court.

Smashes off the back wall.

We must mention a specific situation that can occur in amateur paddle tennis and many of us may not know about it.

This is the case of a smash off the back wall that is going to go out of bounds but the smash hitter, after hitting the ball, touches the net.

In this case, it is very important to know that when the net is touched, there is a normative margin of conflict, as the point goes to the player who touched the net if the ball has already exceeded a height of 4 meters, that is, if when hitting the smash, the player avoids touching the net until the ball goes past the back of the court, the point would be valid, even if the net is touched afterwards, while if the player touches the net before the ball exceeds 4 meters, the point goes to the opponent.

76

Three-wall shots.

In this case, it will depend on the rule whether the outside shot is authorized or not, meaning if the outside shot is authorized, the point is not valid until it bounces out of the court and therefore concludes.

These situations may occur in amateur paddle tennis since it is not so complicated for a player to reach a shot and hit it by bouncing it out of the court three or four times, so it is important to keep in mind.

However, the difficult part will be to determine when the net is touched, i.e., before or after it passes the fence in the case of three or four without an outside shot, or if it is touched before bouncing out of the court in the case of an outside shot.

77

Touching the opponent's court.

Ale Galán almost reached the end of the 10-meter legal limit and returned the ball, but the referee invalidated the point as he touched the fence on the opposite side, meaning we can go out and return the ball, but for it to be valid, we cannot touch the opponent's court as it invalidates the play.

Thanks to a reader who is a specialist in the field, we must clarify that this last case only happens in the World Paddle Tennis Tour.

If you lean on the fence from the outside of your opponents' side, it is considered a fault, but it is a WPT-specific rule.

According to the literal interpretation of the regulations, the outside zone is "neutral."

So, you could lean on (but not grip) the fence from the outside, as you would be touching the "neutral zone."

The problem arose a few seasons ago when Eli Amatriaín literally grabbed onto the fence, and then by touching the opponent's court from the inside, it would be an invalidated play.

Therefore, we predict that soon the international paddle tennis rule will also change, following the simplicity of the WPT rule, which avoids interpretation errors.

If you grip the mesh from the outside, your fingers in the inside court touch the opponent's playing area.

78

Once the ball goes out of the court, the point concludes, and the following rules must be followed:

-If the ball bounces twice on the opponent's court before going out of the court, the point is considered for the opposing team.

-If the ball hits a player's body before going out of the court, the point is considered for the opposing team.

-If the ball goes out of the court after bouncing on the opponent's court and re-enters the court but does not bounce inside and goes out again, the point is considered for the opposing team that did not touch the ball.

-If the ball goes out of the court and does not meet any of the above conditions, the point is repeated.

79

Positive thoughts are a powerful tool for improving performance in paddle tennis and any other sport.

Some examples of positive thoughts that can help improve performance include:

- **"I am more important than any obstacle"**: This thought helps to maintain focus on oneself and what can be controlled, rather than being distracted by external obstacles that can affect the game.

- **"I want to be the best version of myself"**: This thought inspires personal growth and continuous improvement, which helps to maintain motivation and continue striving to achieve goals.

- **"There is always a plan B, I will reach my goal no matter what!"**: This thought helps to maintain a positive attitude towards obstacles and to find alternative solutions to achieve goals.

- **"Luck does not exist, it depends on me"**: This thought helps to take responsibility for one's own performance and to maintain focus on effort and dedication rather than relying on external factors.

- **"The most important thing is to learn and continue improving day by day"**: This thought helps to maintain a learning attitude and to seek opportunities for improvement, which helps to maintain motivation and continue advancing in the game.

80

These are some tips to get the most out of your paddle tennis training:

-Create habits: Establish a regular schedule for your training and stick to it.

-Be disciplined: Try to maintain focus and concentration during your training, and avoid unnecessary distractions.

-Take care of your nutrition and hydration: Make sure you are well-fed and hydrated before, during, and after your training.

-Have a plan with short, medium, and long-term goals: Define your goals for training and work consistently to achieve them.

-Think positive: Maintain a positive attitude focused on progress and improvement.

-Trust yourself: Believe in your abilities and in your ability to overcome any obstacle.

-Take necessary actions to prevent injuries: Keep your body in good condition and pay attention to injuries by doing necessary stretching and warm-ups.

- Dedicate time to recovery and rest: Allow your body to recover properly after each training session.

- Above all, enjoy the sport: Make sure paddle tennis remains a fun and enjoyable activity, enjoying every moment of training and play.

81

What to analyze in our rivals?

-Are our rivals right-handed or left-handed?

-What height do they have?

-Do they use flat or spin shots?

-What physical conditions do they possess?

-Are their movements and/or footwork fluid?

-How are the grips on their groundstrokes?

-Where do they feel more comfortable, at the net or at the baseline?

-How well do they "relate" to the walls?

-Do we notice any technical deficiency in their shots?

-And their posture, is it adequate, low center of gravity or do they simply remain upright?

-How is the relationship and communication between them, correct?

-Do they overuse any particular shot?

-Do they protect their backhand side?

-When they come to the net, do they excessively stick to it?

82

Parallel smash.

We could say that this is the "normal smash"
that we all know, the power or finishing smash.

The goal is to try to make the ball
come back to our court.

Since we are going to hit with the greatest force,
it is important to get to the shot comfortably.

This type of smash has a big disadvantage if we
are not able to get the ball back to our court.

The ball would be easy to attack for the
opponent and almost at net height.

This means that you have lost the initiative
and probably the point.

If you realize that it could happen,
run to the back of the court!

We also have to pay attention to the
condition of the balls for this shot.

If they have played a few matches or are wet...
don't try it, you will surely lose the net.

83

Strong smash "for short players" (parallel or cross-court).

The idea is to let the ball drop a bit more than in the previous smash, with the objective of accelerating the ball, not bringing it back to your court.

By hitting hard and low, we put more acceleration on the ball, so it should be done when the opponents are at the back of the court, and thus be able to surprise them.

Alternating this type of smash with the next one I will explain will drive opponents crazy.

We have the option of hitting to the body, so the opponent has to move aside and then go for the ball, but here ethics come into play.

If we hit parallel, it would be important to do so, or the opponent will easily reach the ball.

Another option is to hit cross-court to the double wall, here it will be important not to hit anything high or it will bounce a lot.

84

The peak shot.

As a pressure weapon, the peak shot is a very effective technique in paddle tennis, since its main objective is to create confusion in the opponent, thus generating a situation of pressure that can lead to an error and point.

To execute the peak shot, it is important to look for a closed angle and make a cross shot, with a medium speed and a good dose of spin.

Ideally, the ball should fall right in the peak area, which is the point where the wall and fence meet at the corners of the court.

It is important to keep in mind that, being a technique that seeks to generate pressure on the opponent, the goal is not so much to directly score the point, but rather to force the opponent to make an error or a defensive shot that allows the player executing the shot to take the initiative in the point.

The peak shot requires some patience and skill to control the direction and speed of the ball.

In addition, it is important to note that, being a very effective technique, the opponent may be prepared for it and try to anticipate it, so it is important to vary the tactics and not overuse the peak shot.

85

Defensive smash.

During the game, when we are in an attacking position (at the net), our opponents will try to take the initiative by launching lobs.

These will not always surpass us, so we can take a few steps back to hit the ball.

Our smash, due to these adjustment steps, will be forced and probably hit from behind the midcourt line.

When hitting under pressure, the smash should be slow and cross, to quickly return to the net and continue attacking.

Many times, what is most difficult about this shot is getting back to the net after hitting it.

If you can't do it, because you're tired, it's better to let the lob pass and go back to defend calmly.

The worst thing we can do is stay in the midcourt.

86

Getting the ball out of the court (hitting it out for 4).

When we are at the net and the opponent sends us an "easy ball" (they leave it close to the net), we can move forward and hit a strong smash aiming for the bounce close to the net so that the ball goes out of the court.

The secret is to move forward at the right moment and make a good wrist turn.

If you don't move forward, you run the risk of the ball hitting the net.

Hitting it out for 4 means that we hit the ball, it bounces on the ground and goes out of the court at the back, where the wall + fence measures 4 meters.

87

The shot to send it out by 3 meters.

It is a technique used mainly to surprise the
opponent and score a direct point.

It is a shot primarily executed from the right side of the court
by left-handed or backhand players, as it allows them
to access an angle to make the shot.

The goal of this shot is to make the ball bounce off the
back wall and exit through the side of the court
known as the 3 meters.

To do so, it is necessary to execute a lifted and cross-court
shot to make the ball go in the right direction.

This shot requires great technique and precision, as if the ball
does not go in the correct direction, it can stay in the center
of the court and facilitate the opponent's counterattack.

For this reason, it is a shot that should only be used by
experienced players with good mastery of the technique.

It is also important to consider that this shot can be risky in
certain situations, as if not executed correctly, it can lead
to a fault or an easy point for the opponent.

Therefore, it is necessary to carefully evaluate the situation
and the opponent's position before making this type of shot.

88

Hitting the ball with side spin on the wall.

Here, the goal is to execute a cross-court shot and make the ball bounce off the wall in an unpredictable way to confuse the opponent.

To execute it, we must imagine the ball as a clock and hit it at the three o'clock position.

In this shot, we must be careful with the force, as hitting it too hard can make the ball bounce and give the opponent time to adjust their movement.

The technique of this shot is very similar to the shot to send it out by 3, but the power would be lower and aiming for the side wall to make the ball die at the end of the court.

In high-level play, it is perfect to alternate between this shot and the shot to send it out by 3.

89

The viper and the lob.

These are two very important shots in paddle tennis and can be very effective in winning points.

The viper is a very aggressive shot executed when the ball comes high and close to the net.

It consists of a cut shot, in which a wrist turn is made just before impact, making the ball come out with a spin that takes it down.

In this way, the ball gains speed and drops quickly, making it difficult for the opponent to return.

On the other hand, the lob is a shot used as a continuation of a ball that bounces off the wall after the opponent's shot.

Its goal is to return the ball without it going too high, to prevent the opponent from making a smash or a shot.

The technique consists of hitting the ball with a smooth and wide movement, with the racket in a horizontal position and the hands apart.

Depending on the situation, a defensive or offensive lob can be executed, in which the goal is to define the point.

It is important to note that these shots require good technique and practice to execute them effectively.

It is also crucial to read the trajectory of the ball well and choose the appropriate moment to execute the shot.

90

Exercises to learn and improve the lifted forehand.

- We practice the lifted forehand shot after a lateral displacement.

- The shot is executed after a diagonal displacement. In the previous exercises, directional objectives could be included: hitting to the net, hitting parallel, cross-court, etc.

- We combine the lifted forehand exercise with an attacking cut volley, so the player will have to change their grip.

- We combine the normal lifted forehand shot with a lifted wall outlet. This shot is perfect for hitting a drop shot at the opponent's feet and surprising them.

- We will perform a combination of all the practiced shots. Lifted forehand, attacking volley, and lifted wall outlet. This forces the player to change their grip again according to the shot to be executed.

91

Characteristics of players who can attack from the back of the court.

This will apply to:

- Fast players.

- Players who have a better volley than smash.

- Players who feel more comfortable at the net than at the back because they may not have a good defense.

On the other hand, this way of playing may be the only possibility for attack for players who do not have good physical fitness or an age where they no longer have the mobility to maintain a good attacking game at the net where greater physical exertion is required.

With this way of playing, they will only spend energy when attacking and not lose it at the net by stepping back to smash and making all the previous shots in the net until they make contact with a defining shot.

92

Attacking from the back of the court with high-speed shots.

It is a commonly used strategy in paddle tennis, as it seeks
to destabilize the opponent and generate
opportunities to win the net.

The forehand and backhand are the most used
shots to attack from the back.

It is important to vary the direction of the shot and also hit the
opponent's body so that they cannot respond comfortably.

In addition, you can choose to hit the shot with topspin so
that the ball bounces high and is difficult to respond to.

Another option for attacking from the back
is to use the high wall outlet.

This play occurs after the ball has bounced off
the wall and comes back to the player.

At this point, you can take advantage of the opportunity
to make a high-speed shot, either flat or with slice,
and generate a bad volley from the opponent.

It is important to keep in mind that attacking from the back
also carries some risk, as a poorly executed shot can
result in an unforced error and lose the point.

Therefore, it is necessary to be selective when choosing when
to attack and always consider the situation of the game.

**Attack from the backcourt by playing
a drop shot or soft shot.**

These are low and slow shots that fall
in front of the opponents.

The characteristics they should have are:

- That our shot (dink) passes close to the net
to ensure that the opponent cannot volley the
ball above the net height, avoiding any
possibility of playing an offensive volley.

- That they are slow shots to give us time to
run behind our ball towards the net and reach a
good attacking position by the time the
opponent executes their shot, in other words,
to be able to enter the net. In this play, we
must run to the net behind our shot since the
speed of our ball will give us time to get closer
to the net. In the case of slow or tired players,
they should perform a 3/4 court volley and
move up to the net in 2 steps.

94

Attack from the backcourt: Moving up to volley the opponent's uncomfortable smash.

This is one of the most complex plays as it requires:

- Decision.

- Speed to reach the net.

- Good volley and reflexes.

- Choosing the opponent and the right moment very well.

Tactically, it can be used when playing against opponents who do not have a very powerful smash and variations against passed lobs.

Generally, these are players who have a very secure and well-directed overhead smash, crosscourt, and with a good direction to keep us controlled at the back without giving us rebounds that can facilitate the counterattack, meaning they have us at the back and take advantage of the first mistake we make to finish the point.

This is where it is convenient to move up to volley the smash, but only when we execute a good lob making the opponent have to execute a very uncomfortable smash, and where we have previously observed throughout the match that he is very repetitive with the smash from that position so we can anticipate the ball he will play and thus shorten the court we have to cover.

95

What do you need to become a professional paddle tennis player?

You might think that the first step is to have a good paddle tennis coach, but this would actually be the second step, as before anything else, you should have a partner to play paddle tennis with whom you complement inside the court, and it is also important to get along well outside of it.

Remember that tactics between partners are important and will be one of the things you should train.

From here, you will have to spend several hours on the court and just as many off it.

The 5 pillars of the professional paddle tennis player are: Technique, Tactics, Physical Preparation, Mental Training, and Nutrition.

96

**Basic rules for competing at
a professional level.**

-Have a good skill level: To participate in World
Paddle Tennis Tour tournaments, you must
achieve a minimum ranking by winning some
important matches (first within our community
and then at the national level).

-Establish a strong connection with your partner.

-Have a good coach.

-Improve your technique.

-Give importance to physical training.

-Develop effective tactics with your partner.

-Work on the mental aspect of the game.

-Maintain a healthy diet.

-Allocate time for rest.

-Familiarize yourself with your opponents.

97

"Yes, I know how to play tennis, this is easy."

This is one of the neighbor's phrases, although there are others like, "Let's play, I'm going to crush you," because he has been given a new racket and because he remembers playing tennis well.

They are sports from the same family, but with very different characteristics.

The only thing you can rescue from years of tennis is coordination of movements and the relationship with the ball.

The rest is learning from scratch or what is even more difficult, changing inherited tennis habits: grip, serve, hitting power, placement, synchronization with your partner...

It is another sport, you have to accept it and learn again.

98

"You'll see my back wall shot."

Students and amateur players insist on
leaving their lives against the back
wall unnecessarily.

The back wall shot is a last resort because
generally you won't make it; because you can
leave the ball mark on your face for life, and
because, assuming you hit it more or less
well, you are sold in the point.

It should only be used when
there is no other option.

Don't look for it.

If you have time, get to the ball, turn and hit
it straight [wall shot] if you want to
stay "alive" in the point.

It is less spectacular, but it is more effective
and safer for preserving your facial features.

99

"Making lobs is for losers."

The typical "passing shot"
that was said in tennis.

Don't be embarrassed to hit them, don't
let yourself be intimidated by
senseless pressure.

The lob takes on a different
meaning in paddle tennis.

It's not just a defensive shot, it's the
beginning of an attack; it's a high ball to the
back of the court that can die on the wall,
that's difficult to return; it's making your
opponent back up; it's winning the court;
it's putting pressure on them; it's a shot
as respectable as any other and, of course,
much more effective than the back wall shot.

Whoever dominates the lob has
a lot to gain in this game.

100

"Just let me handle it, I'll blast it."

We all have a friend who uses paddle tennis
to release the tensions of the week.

Once, when they still have air, it works: they blast
it and take it out of the court, but it's
only 1 or 2 out of 10 chances.

The rest end up in the net, they don't hit it, they leave
it perfect for you to return, they crack the back
wall or send it onto the highway.

The problem with this "buddy," who probably played
tennis or fronton, is that they feel powerful with a
manageable racket that sends the ball flying, in
a court of reduced dimensions and with a
game that encourages finishing.

But friend, the wall always returns that ball to us.

So, we have to change the concept: paddle tennis is
about keeping the point alive, demanding from the
opponent, making fewer mistakes than the other,
wearing them down, attacking with purpose
and not just hitting the ball hard.

101

A paddle tennis joke.

One day I woke up early, got dressed slowly, made coffee, grabbed my paddle tennis bag, quietly went to the garage and proceeded to take the car out of the garage in a torrential rain.

The whole street was flooded, the freezing wind was blowing at 100 km/h and several trees had fallen.

I drove the car back into the garage, turned on the radio and found out that the bad weather was going to last all day.

I went back into my house, quietly undressed and slid into bed.

Slowly I snuggled up against my wife's back and whispered in her ear: "The weather outside is terrible."

She half asleep replied: "I know, can you believe that my idiot husband went to play paddle tennis?"

If you have enjoyed the curiosities of paddle tennis presented in this book, we would like to ask you to share a review on Amazon.

Your opinion is very valuable to us and to other paddle tennis enthusiasts who are looking to have fun and learn new knowledge.

We understand that leaving a comment can be a tedious process, but we ask you to take a few minutes of your time to share your thoughts and opinions with us.

Your support is very important to us and it helps us continue creating quality content for fans of this incredible sport.

We appreciate your support and hope that you have enjoyed reading our book as much as we enjoyed writing it.

Thank you for sharing your experience with us!

★ ★ ★ ★ ★